101+

Empowering Quotes

For New Entrepreneurs

Dr. Shelly Cameron

Dedicated to

Nordia, Kevin, RJ & Ashleigh

$\mathcal{I}$ntroduction

People often say that motivation doesn't last. Well, neither does bathing - that's why we recommend it daily. – Zig Ziglar

Startup and Never Stop

Do you know why some people succeed while others don't? It's simple. They never give up. Successful people press on when the going gets tough and they become discouraged. J. K. Rowling was rejected by 12 publishers before Harry Potter and The Philosopher's Stone was accepted. Walt Disney was turned down 302 times before he got financing to create Disneyland. Albert Einstein did not speak until he was four and did not read until seven. He went on to win a Nobel Prize and became the guru of modern physics.

Why Motivational Quotes for New Entrepreneurs?

Because **Motivation is the key to Success**. With over 25 Million Americans starting or running new businesses, entrepreneurship has become incredibly attractive, yet extremely difficult to sustain. Adding to the excitement, the Gig Economy's Freelancers comprise over 35 percent of the U.S. Workforce. Even with the traits of fearlessness, risk-taking, passion, resilience, and creativity, difficulties arise, and Entrepreneurs need to keep going. That's where a boost of inspiration comes in. Motivational Speakers the likes of Les Brown, Tony Robins, Nick Vujicic, Zig Zigler, and Brian Tracy engage the minds and hearts of people to achieve their higher purpose.

In 2017, my love of quotes inspired me to publish the first edition of **Motivational Quotes to Boost Your Success** and was well received as business owners, salespersons, and those interested in their personal development chewed on it daily. Pioneer, Marc Anderson said it best in his own take on quotes, *"I've had many 'aha' moments, where I've read it and thought...wow, that's exactly how I feel!"*

So, enjoy this little book of Motivation. Offer it as a Corporate or personal Gift and sow seeds of encouragement to a deserving soul today.

Cheers to your Success!

Everything started as nothing.

– Ben Weissenstein

$\mathcal{F}$ear is not real. The only place that fear can exist is in our thoughts of the future. It is a product of our imagination, causing us to fear things that do not at present and may not ever exist. That is near insanity. Do not misunderstand me danger is very real but fear is a choice.

– Will Smith

Leap. The net will appear.

– Julia Cameron

All you need to know is

that it's possible.

– Wolf

Success: it's Not their Dream.

It's yours. Never Give Up.

– Kevin Hart

Whatever you want to do, just

start where you are.

You can't wish that it's going to

be perfect in the beginning. And

when you start, you begin to see

all the directions you can go, all

the possibilities become available.

But if you never start, you never

see it.

– Pat Chin

$\mathcal{N}$ever cut a tree down in the wintertime. Never make a negative decision in the low time. Never make your most important decisions when you are in your worst moods. Wait. Be patient. The storm will pass. The spring will come.

– Robert H. Schuller

Your time is limited.

Don't waste it living someone

else's life.

– Melodie Beattie

If you're not a risk taker, you
should get the hell out of business.

– Ray Kroc

Always deliver more than expected.

– Larry Page

You have to do what you have to do until you can do what you want to do.

– Oprah Winfrey

The life you've led doesn't have to be the only life you have.

– Anna Quindlen

Never give up a dream

because of the time it will take to

accomplish it.

– unknown

What appears to be the end of the road may simply be a bend in the road.

– Robert H. Schuller

Do, or do not. There is no try.

– Jedi Master

If you want to do it, Do

it now.

– Catharine Cook

There's nothing wrong with staying small. You can do big things with a small team.

– Jason Fried

Ideas are easy. Implementation

is hard.

– Guy Kawasaki

Life's too short to learn

from your own mistakes.

Learn from others.

– unknown

$\mathscr{T}$he best time to plant a tree

was 20 years ago. The second-best

time is now.

– Chinese proverb

Twenty years from now, you will be more disappointed by the things that you didn't do than by the ones you did do. So, throw off the bowlines, sail away from safe harbor, catch the trade winds in yours. Explore. Dream. Discover.

– Mark Twain

A person *who never made a mistake never tried anything new.*

– Albert Einstein

I'd rather attempt to do
something great and fail than to
do nothing and succeed.

– Robert H. Schuller

It is important to remember that we cannot become what we need to be by remaining what we are.

– Max De Pree

As you move towards a dream,

the dream moves towards you.

Take the step. Make that move

now.

– Julia Cameron

Your Doubts creates

mountains. Your actions

Move them.

– Mel Robbins

Nothing is as painful as being stuck where you do not belong. It's time. Move on.

– N.R. Nanyana Murthy

Understanding your failures and practice in overcoming obstacles are invaluable on the path to sustainable entrepreneurial success.

– Roxanne Valies

Success means surrounding yourself with like-minded and success-driven people.

– Nordia Cameron-Cunningham

Failure will never overtake you

if your determination to Succeed is

strong enough.

– Og Mandino

$\mathcal{Y}$ou can't Decide by Thinking.

You Decide by Doing.

– Ricci

Learn from each other.

Passion, skill and talent. That's

how you get success.

– Monique Calder

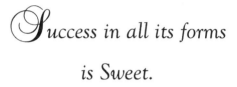

Success in all its forms is Sweet.

– Dr. Shelly Cameron

Don't ask yourself what the

world needs;

ask yourself what makes you come

alive, then go do that

– Margie Warrell

$\mathcal{R}$isk taking without
ability leads to frustration
and continual failure.
Risk taking with ability leads to
increased learning and success

– John Maxwell

Don't cling to a mistake because you took a long time making it.

– Aubrey De Graf

What's the most important step a man can take? The Next one.

– Bandon Sanderson

Focus on value: The successful business is the one that creates and articulates clear value for their customers. It's always important to ask yourself what value you are creating and does your market understand and appreciate your value.

– Gregory Turner

I don't put myself in a box so why would I try to fit in yours?

– Camacho Roberts

Every morning greet the day with gratefulness. The course has been set. Run the race and win.

– Bridget King

$\mathcal{C}$limb the mountain so that
you may see the world not so that
the world may see you.

– David McCullough

Try it. Fail? Try Again. Never Give Up.

– Dr. Shelly Cameron

$\mathcal{I}$t's not what you look at that
matters, it's what you see.

– Henry David Thoreau

Your Smile is your logo, your personality is your business card, how you leave others feeling after an experience with you becomes your trademark.

– The Fit Bunch

$\mathcal{T}$he fears we don't face become

our limit.

– Robin Sharda

Ambition is the Path

to Success.

Persistence is the vehicle

you arrive in.

– Bill Bradley

Even nice things don't make you happy when you're tired.

– Jo Brand

The life you've led doesn't have to be the only life you have.

– Anna Quindlen

Even if you cannot change the people around you, you can change the people you're around.

– R.T. Bennett

You can't cross the sea merely by standing and staring at the water.

– Rabindranath Tagone

You can't control the past but

you can control where you go next.

– Kirsten Hubbard

Know and fulfil your purpose.

– Kevin Cameron

It all begins and ends in your mind. What you give power to, has power over you if you allow it.

– Leon Brown

Success is a matter of hanging

on after others have let go.

– William Fearger

It's better to be at the bottom of the ladder you want to climb than at the top of the one you don't.

– Stephen King

The truth hurts, but the lies hurt more.

– Bridget King

You can't start the next chapter
if you keep re-reading the last.

– Anonymous

$\mathcal{L}$et bygones be bygones. Don't live in the past lane.

– Samantha Ettus

*Y*our Doubts

creates mountains.

Your actions Move them.

– Mel Robbins

$\mathcal{Q}$uit *talking and begin doing.*

– Walt Disney

$\mathcal{R}$emember why you started

– Chris Burkmenn

An entrepreneur tends to bite off a little more than he can chew hoping he'll quickly learn how to chew it.

– Roy Ash

A ship in harbor is safe. But that's not what it's built for.

– John A. Shedd

If you don't have big dreams and goals. You'll end up working for someone that does.

– Unknown

Don't worry about failure; you only have to be right once.

– Drew Houston

Someone is sitting in the shade today because someone planted a tree a long time ago.

– Warren Buffett

Knowledge without action

is meaningless.

– Abu Bakr

Growth is painful. Change is faithful. Nothing is as painful as staying stuck where you do not belong.

– N.R. Nanyana Murthy

Each person holds so much Power within themselves that needs to be let out. Sometimes they need a little nudge, a little direction, a little coaching and the greatest things can happen.

– Pete Carroll

If you think you can,

you're right

– Henry Ford.

A single dream is more powerful than a thousand realities. Never Give Up on your dream.

– J.R.R. Tolkien

Things Change. Move on.

– Dr. Shelly Cameron

When it comes to the future, there are three kinds of people. Those who let it happen; those who make it happen; and those who wonder what happened.

– John M Richardson, Jr.

$\mathcal{S}$uccess is liking yourself, liking what you do and liking how you do it.

– Maya Angelou

Whatever you fear most, has no power. It's your fear that has the power.

– Oprah Winfrey

Don't ask yourself what the world needs; ask yourself what makes you come alive, then go do that

– Margie Warrell

The further away you are from where you started, the closer you get to where you belong.

– Anonymous

$\mathcal{W}$hen everything seems to be going against you, remember that the airplane takes off against the wind, not with it.

– Henry Ford

Authenticity creates presence, confidence and influence.

– Matthew Jones

Begin with the End in mind.

– Steven Covey

There's little success where there's little laughter.

– Andrew Carnegie

Say no: A common mistake made by entrepreneurs is to say 'yes' to every opportunity presented to them. Declutter your schedule by focusing on no more than 3 things you need to do to meet your goal. Less is more.

– Gregory Turner

Don't worry about failures.

Worry about the chances you miss

when you don't even try.

– Jack Canfield

Thoughts do not equal action.

Think it. Ink it. Do it.

– Dr. Shelly Cameron

$\mathcal{K}$eep your fears to yourself but

share your courage with others.

– Robert Louis Stevenson

Great works are performed not by strength. But by perseverance.

– Samuel Johnson

Start by doing what's necessary; then do what's possible; and suddenly you are doing the impossible.

– Francis of Assisi

Continually Investing in the

Success of Others is what will

Lead to your Success.

– Chris Hadfield

One small crack doesn't mean you're broken. It means you were tested and you didn't fall apart.

– Linda Paindexter

Failure will never overtake you if your determination to Succeed is strong enough.

– Og Mandino

One's Destination is never a place, but always a new way of seeing things.

– Henry Miller

When you get to a tight place, and everything goes against you, till you seem as if you couldn't hold on a minute longer, never give up then, for that's just the place and time that the tide'll turn.

– Harriet Beecher Stowe

Opportunity is found when you look beyond the familiar and see the possible.

– unknown

The people who are most successful are the ones who are doing what they love.

– Warren Buffet

As you become successful, be prepared for the haters, but don't let it stop you. Enjoy your success.

– Dr. Shelly Cameron

When you try to fit in you'll disappear. Be different.

– Unknown

When you feel discouraged about your business idea, because there's so many people around you doing the same thing, go to the grocery store and look down the bread aisle. Same idea 15+ companies selling the same thing! We all can eat. Don't doubt your ability.

– The Shade Room.

$\mathcal{R}$isk-taking *without ability*

leads to frustration and

continual failure. Risk-taking

with ability leads to increased

learning and success.

– John Maxwell

Start Doing what is Necessary.

Then Do what's Possible. Then

Suddenly, you're Doing the

Impossible.

– St. Francis of Assisi

Growth. There are no Mistakes, Only Lessons. Reflect and Learn.

– John Maxwell

Quit Worrying. If it was supposed to be yours, You Would Have Gotten it. Keep Trusting.

– Dr. Shelly Cameron

Go Above or Beyond

the Expected.

– Scott Burrows

Life Shrinks or Expands in

relation to your Courage.

– Anais Nin

I can either cross the street or I can keep waiting for another few years of green lights to go by.

– Camryn Maheim

Our Deepest Fear should not be of Failure but of Succeeding in Life at Things that Don't Really Matter.

– Chan

Those who drink the water must remember those who dug the well.

– Chinese Proverb

If you don't go after what you want, you'll never have it. If you don't ask, the answer is always no. If you don't step forward, you will always be in the same place.

– Nora Roberts

Monotony is the awful reward

of the careful.

– A.G. Buckham

Look Ahead. The Future's Bright.

– Dr. Shelly Cameron

The flower which is single need not envy the thorns that are numerous.

– Rabindranath Tagore

You can't cross the sea merely by standing and staring at the water. Make that Move

– Rabindranath Tagore

Goals: Don't allow anyone to tell you it's not possible.

– Howard Schultz

Action is the key to Success.

– Pablo Picasso

Be a River, Not a Reservoir.

– John Maxwell

We cast a shadow on

something wherever we stand.

– E.M. Forster

Sometimes you will just have to do it Afraid.

– Unknown

When Everything is Coming your way, you're probably in the wrong lane. Be wise, Look beyond the Obvious.

– Tom Snyder

$\mathcal{Y}$ou cannot change direction if you are not aware of where you want to go.

– Jim Rohn

Feel the Fear. Do it anyway.

– Susan Jeffers

What you allow is what will Continue.

– Unknown

$\mathcal{M}$istakes, Failures, Regrets.

Don't Carry. Learn from them.

Rise above them.

– Dr. Shelly Cameron

The mind is like water. When it's turbulent it's difficult to see. When it's calm, everything becomes clear.

– Prasad Mahes

You don't have to See the whole staircase, *Just take the First Step.*

– Martin Luther King

You can't depend on your eyes when your imagination is out of focus.

– Mark Twain

The future depends on what you do today.

– Mahatma Ghandi

Where you are may not be where you want to be but hold on. It's all a part of the plan.

– Unknown

Value your time. If you don't, nobody else will.

– Anonymous

If you find that you are the smartest one in the group that you hang with, you need to find a new group. In order to grow, you need to develop. Staying in your comfort zone won't help.

– Michael Dell

Opportunity is found when you look beyond the familiar and see the impossible.

– Anonymous

$\mathcal{T}$he Dream disturbs the sleep.

Make it happen.

– Anonymous

Don't Fear Failure. Fear being in the same place this time next year.

– Unknown

$\mathcal{Y}$ou cannot swim for new
horizons until you have courage to
lose sight of the shore.

– William Faulkner

It's never too late to be what

you might have been.

– George Eliot

*L*ife Rewards those who

take action.

– Brian Tracy

The cave that you Fear holds
the Treasure you Desire.

– Joseph Campbell

No one can make you feel inferior without your consent.

– Eleanor Roosevelt

The Fears We Don't Face

Becomes our Limit.

– Robin Sharda

When you find an idea that you just can't stop thinking about, that's probably a good one to pursue.

– Josh James

It's not about ideas. It's about making ideas happen.

– Scott Belsky

The only thing worse than starting something and failing... is not starting something.

– Seth Godin

The fastest way to change yourself is to hang out with people who are already the way you want to be.

– Reid Hoffman

When Life Throws you Lemons, Make Lemonade.

– R. Berg

Money is not an object: Ask for what you are worth. Never hesitate to ask for what you want. For your ideal customer, money is never an object. Their concern is the value and return on investment. If you articulate this clearly and enthusiastically, money is not an object.

– Gregory Turner

Turn a perceived risk

into an asset."

– Aaron Patzer

$\mathcal{D}$on't wait around for other people to be happy for you. Any happiness you get, you've got to make yourself.

– Alice Walker

It's more effective to do something valuable than to hope a logo or name will say it for you.

– Jason Cohen

Don't be cocky. Don't be flashy. There's always someone better than you.

– Tony Hsieh

Chase the vision, not the money; the money will end up following you.

– Tony Hsieh

Courage Doesn't Always Roar.

Sometimes Courage is the quiet

voice at the end of the day saying,

I'll try again tomorrow.

– Mary Anne Radmacher

If there is no way, create one.

– Jeremy McGilvrey

$\mathcal{D}$on't do it if it has

no purpose.

– Anonymous

People may spend their whole lives climbing the ladder of success only to find, once they reach the top, that the ladder is leaning against the wrong wall.

– Thomas Merton

Dreams come through.

Without that Possibility, Nature

would not incite us to have them.

– John Updike

You have to do what

you *dream of doing even*

while you're afraid.

– Ariana Huffington

Focus on who Christ is and not the crisis.

– Camacho Roberts

When you can't see clearly.
Slow down or even stop. It's
important to get back on track in
the same or different direction. No
surprise. Be wise.

– Dr. Shelly Cameron

It's none of your Business what People think of you. Focus on where you're going.

– Unknown

Those who have a 'why' to live,

can bear with almost any 'how'.

– Viktor Frankl

The only journey is the

one within.

– Rainer Maria Rilke

Don't limit yourself to what other people think you are or should be. Take the limits off. God's thoughts define me.

– Camacho Roberts

Not all storms come to disrupt your life, some come to clear your path.

– Unknown

New Entrepreneur? Like a new born, Nurture and Care for the Business. Consistency is key. Then Growth is sure.

– Dr. Shelly Cameron

You can't cross the sea merely by standing and staring at the water.

– Rabindranath Tagore

Your reputation doesn't follow you. It gets there before you do.

– Bill Crawford

You must expect great things of yourself before you can do them.

– Michael Jordan

About The Author

Dr. Shelly Cameron is an Organizational Leadership Specialist. Through her book **Success Strategies of Immigrant Leaders,** she revealed the results of a Phenomenological study conducted with Nova Southeastern University and published in the Journal of American Academy of Business Cambridge (JAABC) which explored the hidden secrets of successful leaders. She now connects it to those aspiring to achieve. Individuals are challenged to take that first step to accomplish their dreams, goals, and aspirations. As Author, Speaker, and Coach, Dr. Cameron holds Graduate degrees in Organizational Leadership, Health Administration, and Human Resource Development.

An avid believer in Motivation, Dr. Cameron has traveled as far as Kenya, East Africa to share her Passion and its link to Goal Achievement, Entrepreneurship and Personal Development.

She holds firmly to the stance that All Things Are Possible with God.

If You Have Enjoyed This Book

Or If It Has Touched Your Life In Some Way, I would Love to Hear from You.

Please email me at:
scameron@ccahr.com

www.shellycameron.com
www.successfulleaders.net

Books By Dr. Shelly Cameron

- Motivational Quotes To Boost Your Success

- 101+ Empowering Quotes for New Entrepreneurs

- Success Strategies: Want To Succeed? Here's How

- Success Strategies of Immigrant Leaders in The United States

- Success Strategies of Caribbean American Leaders in the United States: Why Some Succeed While Others Don't

- GreenLight: When God Says Go

- The Leadership Challenge: Published in the Journal of American Academy of Business Cambridge (JAABC)